The Warrior Mom's Guide to Homeschooling for the Homegirls

Shaundra M. G. Harris

The Warrior Mom's Guide to Homeschooling for the Homegirls

Real-Life Homeschooling Tips for Single Moms with Chronic Illness

Author Shaundra M. G. Harris

Shaun The Mom Publishing

© 2025 Shaundra M. G. Harris.
All rights reserved.

Paperback ISBN: 978-1-969446-06-1
Hardback ISBN: 978-1-969446-16-0

First Edition

No part of this publication may be reproduced, stored in a retrieval system, or transmitted in any form without written permission from the author, except by reviewers or educators using brief quotations with proper citation.

Publisher Shaun The Mom Publishing

Printed in the United States.

www.warriormomacademy.com

Disclaimer

This book is intended for informational and inspirational purposes only. The content reflects the personal experiences, opinions, and insights of the author and should not be considered a substitute for professional medical, legal, financial, educational, therapeutic, or spiritual advice.

While the author shares tools, tips, and resources that have been personally helpful, every situation is unique. Readers are encouraged to consult with qualified professionals before making decisions regarding health, finances, homeschooling, parenting, estate planning, or other matters discussed in this book.

Some links or references provided may be affiliate links. This means the author may receive a small commission at no extra cost to you if you choose to purchase through those links. These recommendations are made in good faith and only include resources the author personally uses or believes may be helpful.

Any printable templates, checklists, or workbook materials included are for personal use only and may not be distributed, sold, or used commercially without written permission from the author.

The author and publisher expressly disclaim any liability arising directly or indirectly from the use or misuse of any information, tools, or resources included in this book.

For all the warrior moms teaching with love and courage—especially those navigating challenges unseen.

For my awesome children.
Aoki, Layla, Jayden and Nia.

Hello

Welcome to the Academy, Sis

This is your space.
A place for mamas who are doing the most—
with the least—and still showing up for their
kids with love, faith, and grit.

Here in The Warrior Mom Academy, we don't
chase perfection.

We chase purpose.
We rest when we need to.
We celebrate small wins.
We make space for grace.

This book is your toolkit, your cheerleader, and
your reminder that you are not alone.

You're building something powerful—even if it
looks different than you expected.

Let's homeschool with heart, on our terms.

Table of Contents

Introduction 2

    Chapter 1: You Are Already a Teacher 2

    Chapter 2: Homeschooling as a Lifestyle 6

    Chapter 3: Finding Lessons in Everyday Life .. 9

    Chapter 4: The Freedom of Homeschooling .. 12

Part I: Foundations of Homeschooling 15

    Chapter 5: Dear Mom 16

    Chapter 6: Why This Book? 20

    Chapter 7: How to Use This Book 24

    Chapter 8: What Is Homeschooling? 27

    Chapter 9: Homeschooling Laws & Requirements 31

    Chapter 10: Homeschool Philosophies 35

    Chapter 11: Finding Your Path......................41

Part II: Planning Your Homeschool.......... 44

    Chapter 12: Creating a Vision—What Matters Most? 45

    Chapter 13: Setting Realistic Goals (Especially with Chronic Illness)..................................... 48

Chapter 14: Choosing Curriculum — A Guide for the Overwhelmed 52

Chapter 15: Creating a Flexible Schedule 55

Chapter 16: How to Track Progress (Without Burning Out) 58

Part III: Homeschooling with Chronic Illness 61

Chapter 17: You Matter Too: 62

Self-Care for the Homeschooling Mom 62

Chapter 18: Energy Management & Spoon Theory for Homeschoolers 66

Chapter 19: Planning for Low-Energy or Flare Days 69

Chapter 20: Building a Support System 72

Chapter 21: Teaching Your Kids While Teaching Resilience 75

Part IV: Creating the Learning Environment 78

Chapter 22: Setting Up a Homeschool Space. 79

Chapter 23: Homeschooling Multiple Ages or Special Needs 82

Chapter 24: Tech Tools, Apps, and Resources 85

Chapter 25: Incorporating Life Skills, Hobbies, and Rest 88

Part V: Teaching Strategies for Real Life .. 92

Chapter 26: When You're the Teacher and the Nurse: Combining Roles 93

Chapter 27: Teaching Without a Textbook: Creative, Hands-On, or Project-Based Learning 96

Chapter 28: Embracing Educational Flexibility 100

Chapter 29: Outsourcing Subjects 103

Part VI: Socialization & Emotional Health 106

Chapter 30: Helping Kids Make Friends (Even If You're Mostly Home) 107

Chapter 31: Handling Criticism and Doubts from Others 110

Chapter 32: Supporting Your Child's Mental Health & Emotions 112

Chapter 33: Celebrating Progress Without Comparison 115

Part VII: Navigating Hard Days & Burnout 117

Chapter 34: Recognizing Burnout Early 118

Chapter 35: Simple Plans for Hard Weeks .. 120

Chapter 36: Grace Over Guilt: You Are Enough 122

Chapter 37: Emergency Plans for Flare-Ups or Hospitalizations 124

Part VIII: Long-Term Homeschooling 126

Chapter 38: Reevaluating Each Year: Stay, Pause, or Pivot? 127

Chapter 39: High School at Home: Transcripts, Credits, & Graduation 129

Chapter 40: College, Trade School, or Alternative Paths 131

Chapter 41: What If I Can't Continue? Planning for Transition 133

Part IX: Inspiration & Resources 136

Chapter 42: Real Moms' Stories: Homeschooling Through Illness 137

Chapter 43: Favorite Curricula by Energy Level 139

Chapter 44: Books, Podcasts, and Online Communities 141

Chapter 45: Printable Templates: Planners, Checklists, Daily Logs................................143

You Were Made for This.............................145

Encouragement for the Journey Ahead........146

Scriptures for Teaching & Patience..........*147*

Book Club & Reflection Questions............ *148*

Glossary of Key Terms............................ *149*

Resources..*154*

The Warrior Mom's Guide™ Book Series.*156*

Acknowledgments...................................*159*

About the Author *160*

Introduction

Chapter 1: You Are Already a Teacher

Hey Y'all, Hey

So, I've been homeschooling for over 20 years now—because let's be honest, teaching starts at birth. From the moment you bring your little one home, you automatically become their first teacher.

They learn from your words, your habits, your love, and even your struggles. Teaching your kids how to learn is just as important as the lessons themselves.

I've juggled lesson plans with hospital visits, taught phonics while managing chronic pain, and still pressed forward—not because it was easy, but because it was possible.

Whether you choose homeschool, private school, or public school, one thing is true: you are your child's first teacher.

One of my children is now finishing college. I've got a high schooler, a middle schooler, and another about to enter middle school—and I want you to know: this path is possible.

Not perfect. But possible.

This book is written to guide, uplift, and equip you for the journey ahead—one grace-filled day at a time.

🦋 Reflection | Affirmation | Prayer | Action

You Are Already a Teacher

Reflection Questions

1. When did you first realize you were your child's first teacher?
2. How do you already see yourself shaping your child's learning at home?
3. What strengths or habits do you bring to your child's education?

Affirmation

I am my child's first and most important teacher.
I already carry wisdom and experience that my child needs.
God has trusted me with this role, and He equips me daily.

Prayer
Lord, thank You for reminding me that I am already teaching my children every day.

Help me to see the little moments as learning opportunities, and give me grace when I doubt myself.

Let me walk boldly in this role, knowing You are guiding me. Amen.

Action Steps

- Write down three everyday activities you already teach your child through.
- Choose one scripture to remind yourself that you are equipped.
- Start calling yourself "Teacher Mom" this week to shift your mindset.

Chapter 2: Homeschooling as a Lifestyle

Homeschooling is more than an educational choice—it's a lifestyle.

A home-style.

It shapes your routines, your habits, and often your sense of self.

In the beginning, our days were messy. I was juggling a newborn, special needs toddler, elementary and middle school, work, and hospital visits.

But over time, the flow came. Our family rhythm found its beat. Structure doesn't arrive overnight, but there is joy in creating it.

When I first started full-time homeschooling, I didn't feel qualified. As a high school dropout with a GED, I doubted myself. I worried about finances. I feared giving up stability. But God had a plan—even in my brokenness.

I've homeschooled through overnight work shifts, chronic illness, heartbreak, surgeries, and setbacks. There were days I thought about quitting. But prayer anchored me, and I remembered:

it's not about perfection, it's about progress.

Reflection | Affirmation | Prayer | Action

Homeschooling as a Lifestyle

Reflection Questions
1. What fears do you have about your qualifications as a homeschooling parent?
2. How does your current lifestyle support—or challenge—homeschooling?
3. What kind of daily flow do you want for your family?

Affirmation
I am qualified to teach my children because God equips me.
My family's rhythm may not look like others, but it is ours.
We are building a lifestyle of love, faith, and resilience.

Prayer
Lord, help me embrace homeschooling as a way of life, not just a school choice.

When I feel unqualified, remind me that You call and equip those You choose.

Bring peace to our home and rhythm to our days. Amen.

Action Steps
- Identify one area of your daily routine that could shift into a smoother rhythm.
- Journal the ways God has already equipped you to homeschool.
- Try one small change this week (bedtime routine, meal prep, or study time) to bring more peace into your flow.

Chapter 3: Finding Lessons in Everyday Life

When I couldn't rely on partners, finances, or even my own health, I turned everyday life into school.

Cleaning the fridge became a lesson in science and responsibility. Grocery shopping turned into budgeting and nutrition class. Cooking taught fractions and teamwork.

I built our own WWJD course to help my son and daughters grow in Christlike character. I designed courses on emotions, self-regulation, and even puberty to help me teach in a way my father is teaching me.

I stopped chasing perfection and focused on progress. Homeschooling gave me the freedom to teach not just academics, but life skills—preparing my children to be thoughtful, capable, faith-filled humans.

And here's the secret:

you don't have to know everything.
You just have to be willing to learn alongside your kids.
The answers are already out there—often in a book, and always in God's Word.

🐾 Reflection | Affirmation | Prayer | Action

Finding Lessons in Everyday Life

Reflection Questions
1. What everyday activities in your home could become teaching moments?
2. How can you include faith lessons in your homeschool?
3. What life skills do you most want your kids to learn?

Affirmation
I see learning opportunities all around me.
My home is a place where faith, life, and academics grow together.
God's wisdom will guide me as I teach my children.

Prayer
Lord, thank You for showing me that learning is everywhere.

Help me see the small, ordinary moments as powerful lessons.

Give me creativity to teach both academics and life skills, and wisdom to keep You at the center of it all. Amen.

Action Steps
- Choose one household task and turn it into a learning activity this week.
- Select one scripture to teach your children as part of "real life" learning.
- Start a family "life skills list" and check things off as they learn.

Chapter 4: The Freedom of Homeschooling

Homeschooling gave me something priceless: time with my children that I can never replace.

Through illness, financial struggles, and heartbreak, it kept us close. Over the past few years, our family has changed in size, status, faith, and strength.

I've changed too. In nearly 21 years of mothering, I've been a working mom, a stay-at-home mom, a working-again mom, a very sick and disabled mom, and a divorced mom. I've been almost every kind of mom you can think of. But the best one, of course, is simply being their mom. And by God's grace, I have always been a mom of faith.

Now, as an author-preneur (author and entrepreneur) mom, I see so much more ahead for our family—more adventure, more purpose, and more of the freedom that homeschooling offers. With Wi-Fi and prayer, we can homeschool anywhere—on road trips, at coffee shops, or while visiting the places we read about.

Choosing a consistent curriculum like Time4Learning gave us structure even when I couldn't give 100%. It reminded me that homeschooling isn't about perfection—it's about commitment. You don't need to be perfect to homeschool well. You only need the courage to keep going.

🦬 Reflection | Affirmation | Prayer | Action

The Freedom of Homeschooling

Reflection Questions
1. What freedoms do you hope homeschooling will give your family?
2. How could homeschooling strengthen your connection with your children?
3. What structures or tools could help you stay consistent?

Affirmation
Homeschooling gives my family both freedom and connection.
Even on hard days, I can create stability for my children.
God is with us in every step of this journey.

Prayer
Lord, thank You for the freedom homeschooling gives our family.

Thank You for the chance to learn, travel, and grow together.

Help me find the balance between structure and flexibility.

Keep me encouraged when I feel weak, and remind me that commitment is enough. Amen.

Action Steps
- Write down three freedoms homeschooling could give your family (time, travel, faith, etc.).
- Research one consistent curriculum option as a safety net.
- Plan one "learning on the go" activity (a field trip, library visit, or travel lesson).

Part I: Foundations of Homeschooling

Chapter 5: Dear Mom

Dear Mom,

After hearing a bit of my story in the introduction, I want to pause and write directly to you—mom to mom.

Homeschooling is not just an educational choice; it's a calling, a lifestyle, and a daily act of faith. Before we get into plans and paperwork, I want you to hear this first: You are already enough.

Homeschooling is not reserved for the perfectly organized, perpetually patient mothers you see on social media. It's for real women like you—women who care deeply about their children's future and are willing to learn along the way.

You might be feeling excited, overwhelmed, or unsure. That's okay. I was, too. And I promise, you're not alone.

If you are also managing chronic illness, know that you have permission to do this differently.

You will have days when your energy is gone. You will have moments when you doubt yourself. But you also have a strength inside you—a determination born of loving your kids so fiercely that you'll find a way.

There is no one right way to homeschool. There is only the way that serves your family best.

1. You don't have to recreate public school in your living room.
2. You don't have to prove yourself to anyone.

This is your invitation to trust yourself.

To trust your kids.

And to trust that what you have to offer is more than enough.

🦬 Reflection | Prayer | Affirmation | Action

Dear Mom

Reflection
1. What part of your story are you most proud of?
2. What does "enough" look like for you as a mother and teacher?
3. What does a successful homeschool day feel like in your heart?

Affirmation
I am already enough—right now, just as I am.
I can homeschool my children in a way that honors our unique rhythm, needs, and love.
Every small step I take is a victory in grace.

Prayer
Lord, Thank You for reminding me that I don't have to be perfect to be present.

Help me release the pressure to do it all and embrace the peace of doing what matters most.

When doubt creeps in, remind me that I am equipped by Your grace and empowered by love.

Let me see the beauty in small beginnings and the strength I carry within. Amen.

Action Steps
- Write a letter to yourself from your future self—one year into homeschooling.

  What does she want you to know?

- Choose an affirmation or reminder (e.g., "I am enough," "Grace over guilt") and post it where you'll see it every morning.

Chapter 6: Why This Book?

You've seen how homeschooling shaped my life through challenges and grace.

But why write another homeschool book?

This book is different because it's not just about curriculum and checklists—it's about homeschooling as a mom with chronic illness, as a single mom, as a woman navigating real life.

Because too few talk about the reality of managing a household, teaching your children, and navigating chronic illness all at once.

Too few remind you that your health challenges don't disqualify you.

This book is here to help you blend practicality and compassion—so you can homeschool sustainably, not perfectly.

Even if you don't have a chronic illness, you may still be a single mom, a working mom, or simply a mom who needs permission to go at your own pace.

In these pages, you'll find:
1. Strategies for teaching on low-energy days
2. Ways to include life skills in daily learning
3. Ideas for building a support system
4. Inspiration from other mothers who have walked this road

This book is not about doing everything.
It's about finding what works and letting the rest go.

🦋 Reflection | Prayer | Affirmation | Action

Homeschooling With or Without Chronic Illness

Reflection
1. What are the biggest obstacles you expect to face in homeschooling?
2. How has your health or life situation shaped your approach to parenting?
3. What kind of support would feel most helpful to you right now?

Affirmation
My challenges do not disqualify me—they deepen my wisdom and compassion.
I can create a homeschool experience that supports both my children's learning and my healing.
I move at the pace of grace, not perfection.

Prayer
Dear God, You know every struggle I carry and every hope I hold close.

Guide me as I build a homeschool that reflects who we are and what we need.

Help me release comparison and embrace the freedom to do this differently.

When I am weary, be my strength. When I am

confused, be my clarity.

Surround me with support, and help me trust the path You're helping me build. Amen.

Action Steps
- Make a list of your biggest worries and one small step you can take for each.
- Identify at least one trusted friend, family member, or online community you can lean on.

Chapter 7: How to Use This Book

This book isn't meant to overwhelm you—it's meant to serve you.

You'll notice the same RAPA flow—Reflection, Affirmation, Prayer, Action—throughout.
These aren't just add-ons.
They're here to help you pause, breathe, and apply what you're reading in real time.

Feel free to skip around, write in the margins, or come back to chapters as needed.
- Need help picking a curriculum? Jump ahead to the Planning section.
- Overwhelmed by criticism? Visit the Socialization & Emotional Health section.
- Feeling burned out? Flip to Navigating Hard Days.

Read what you need, when you need it.

Most importantly, give yourself grace.
This is your homeschool, your family, your pace.

🦋 Reflection | Prayer | Affirmation | Action

How to Use This Book

Reflection
1. What part of homeschooling do you feel most confident about?
2. What part do you feel least prepared for?
3. How do you prefer to learn—step by step or jumping around?

Affirmation
I have permission to go at my own pace.
I am allowed to adapt, skip around, and do what works for my family.
I trust myself to find the next right step—one chapter, one choice at a time.

Prayer
Heavenly Father, Thank You for resources that speak to my heart and honor my journey.

Help me to approach this book with openness, grace, and flexibility.

Show me where to start and how to grow from there.

Remind me that this is not a race but a relationship—with my children, my faith, and myself. Amen.

Action Steps
- Make a list of chapters you want to read first.
- Set aside time each week to revisit sections as your needs change.

Chapter 8: What Is Homeschooling?

Homeschooling isn't about replicating the classroom at home—it's about learning as a way of life.

When I first started, I thought homeschooling meant rigid schedules and color-coded binders—but over time, I learned that the most important lessons often happen in unexpected moments—baking bread, solving a problem, or simply talking about life.

Homeschooling is more than "school at home."

It's an educational approach where you, the parent, take primary responsibility for your child's learning.

That might mean following a set curriculum, designing your own lessons, or blending traditional academics with real-life experiences.

Homeschooling is also:
- Flexible – You can tailor learning to your child's strengths, interests, and needs. (And over time, I learned flexibility is a gift).
- Personal – You decide what matters most for your family's values.
- Dynamic – Learning happens everywhere—at the kitchen table, in the yard, at the library, or during a nature walk.

It's not about trying to recreate the public-school experience in your living room.

Homeschooling looks different for every family. For some, it's structured and classical. For others, it's free-form and interest-led.

The beauty is that you get to decide.

🦋 Reflection | Prayer | Affirmation | Action

What Is Homeschooling?

Reflection
1. What does "homeschooling" mean to you right now?
2. What aspects of traditional school do you want to keep, and what do you want to change?
3. How do you hope your child feels about learning at home?

Affirmation
Homeschooling in my home will be guided by love, curiosity, and connection.
I am free to shape our learning in ways that serve our values and our joy.
Learning doesn't have to look like school to be meaningful.

Prayer
God, Thank You for the gift of freedom in how I teach and raise my children.

Help me release rigid ideas of what education "should" be.

Guide me to create a home where learning feels natural, safe, and exciting.

Give me the courage to trust my instincts and the grace to grow as we go. Amen.

Action Steps
- Write your own definition of homeschooling—what it will look and feel like for your family.
- Make a list of spaces in your home where learning naturally happens.
- Talk with your child about what excites them about learning at home.

Chapter 9: Homeschooling Laws & Requirements

Before you dive in, it's important to know your state's laws. I remember the overwhelm of Googling state requirements late at night. You don't have to carry that alone—I'll guide you through the basics.

Homeschooling is legal in all 50 U.S. states, but the rules vary widely. Some states require only a notice of intent, while others expect you to submit curriculum plans, maintain attendance records, or do annual testing.

3 Steps to Get Started:

Step 1: Learn Your State Laws
Visit hslda.org or your state's Department of Education website to find:
- Age requirements
- Notice of intent forms
- Record-keeping rules
- Testing or evaluation requirements

Step 2: File What's Needed
If you must send a notice of intent or affidavit, do so before your child's first day of homeschool. Always keep a copy.

Step 3: Keep Records
Even if minimal documentation is required, maintaining simple records helps if you ever need to

enroll your child in school later.
Keep:
- Attendance logs
- Samples of work
- Progress reports or grades (if applicable)

International Considerations:
If you live outside the U.S., check your country's homeschooling laws. Some countries are supportive; others have restrictions. Look for local homeschool associations or online expat groups for reliable information.

Important: You do not need to be intimidated by paperwork. Start small—one form at a time.

🦋 Reflection | Prayer | Affirmation | Action

Legal Requirements & Registration

Reflection
1. What questions do you have about legal requirements?
2. What part of the registration process feels most stressful?
3. What kind of record-keeping feels realistic for you?

Affirmation
I am capable of learning what I need to know to legally homeschool my children.
I take this one step at a time, with confidence and peace.
My effort to protect and guide my family is sacred work.

Prayer
Lord, As I step into the legal and practical parts of homeschooling, steady my heart.

Give me clarity, patience, and the resources I need to do this well.

Help me not to be overwhelmed by forms or rules, but to see them as tools to protect what matters most.

Surround me with support and help me stay grounded in purpose, not pressure. Amen.

Action Steps
- Visit HSLDA or your state's Department of Education site to learn your requirements.
- Make a checklist of any forms or notices you must submit.
- Set up a simple binder or digital folder to keep records.

Chapter 10: Homeschool Philosophies

Homeschooling is beautifully diverse.

There are countless ways to teach and learn at home, and no single path is the "right" one. Because I've homeschooled through chronic illness, I want to remind you: your way is valid—even if it looks completely different from your neighbor's.

One of the biggest blessings of homeschooling is the freedom to choose your approach.

You can adapt your methods based on your energy levels, your child's interests, your faith, and your season of life.

What works one year (or one month) may change later—and that's okay. Flexibility is not failure; it's wisdom.

Before you pick curriculum or create a daily rhythm, it helps to explore the most common homeschool philosophies.

Each offers a different way to see learning, structure time, and nurture growth.

Popular Approaches to Homeschooling

Traditional / School-at-Home
This approach mirrors public or private school. You follow a structured schedule, complete daily lessons,

and use textbooks or online curriculum.
- Best for: Families who value predictability and clear benchmarks.
- Why it works: It provides stability and accountability, which can help during high-stress or low-energy seasons.
- Keep in mind: It's okay to modify the pace—what matters is understanding, not checking every box.

Charlotte Mason
Rooted in the philosophy of 19th-century educator Charlotte Mason, this method emphasizes living books (rich, story-filled texts), nature walks, art, and the formation of good habits.
- Best for: Families who love literature, beauty, and gentle learning rhythms.
- Why it works: It nurtures the heart and mind together and can be beautifully manageable for moms who need slower, more restful days.

Unschooling
Unschooling removes formal curriculum altogether. Children learn through life experiences, natural curiosity, and pursuing their own interests.
- Best for: Families who value freedom, creativity, and independence.
- Why it works: It fosters self-motivation and deep engagement—but it also requires trust in the process and in your child's innate desire to learn.

Classical
Based on ancient methods of education, the

Classical approach teaches in three stages: Grammar (building knowledge), Logic (understanding relationships between ideas), and Rhetoric (expressing knowledge clearly and persuasively).
- Best for: Families who value structure, critical thinking, and language-based learning.
- Why it works: It creates strong thinkers and communicators—but may need to be simplified or adapted for energy-limited days.

Montessori
Founded by Dr. Maria Montessori, this philosophy emphasizes child-led, hands-on learning. Materials are designed to encourage independence, concentration, and respect for the child's pace.
- Best for: Independent learners and tactile children.
- Why it works: It builds confidence and focus. Even a small "learning shelf" or organized workspace can help your child thrive without constant direction.

Unit Studies
This approach connects all subjects through a single theme or topic. For example, a unit on "Bees" might include reading stories, studying science, making honey recipes, and writing poems.
- Best for: Creative families and multiple-age households.
- Why it works: It saves time and energy by teaching multiple concepts at once—and makes learning feel alive and connected.

Eclectic
This is the "mix-and-match" method, combining elements from different philosophies to fit your family's needs.
- Best for: Moms who value flexibility and personalization.
- Why it works: It's practical, adaptable, and can evolve as your child grows—or as your health and life circumstances shift.

Remember: You don't have to pick just one philosophy.

Many families blend approaches over time, especially as they get to know their child's learning style and their own teaching rhythm.

What matters most is the peace and connection in your home—not how closely you follow someone else's model.
Homeschooling is not about perfection; it's about presence.

🐝 Reflection | Prayer | Affirmation | Action

Understanding Different Homeschooling Philosophies

Reflection
1. Which philosophy feels most aligned with your values and season of life?
2. How does your child naturally explore or express curiosity?
3. What parts of traditional schooling do you want to redefine or release?
4. How can your homeschool philosophy honor both your strengths and your limitations?

Affirmation
There is no one-size-fits-all method—I am free to explore what fits our rhythm and season.
My homeschool doesn't have to look like anyone else's to be powerful and successful.
I trust my child's uniqueness and my ability to lead with love and grace.

Prayer
God, thank You for the variety of ways to learn and grow.

Guide me toward the approach that best fits my child's heart and our family's flow.

Help me to homeschool with peace, flexibility, and joy.

When comparison tries to creep in, remind me that You called me to this path on purpose. Amen.

Action Steps
- Read about at least two homeschooling philosophies and take notes on what stands out.
- Ask your child how they learn best—through reading, doing, seeing, or exploring.
- Circle or highlight the approaches that feel like a natural fit for your home.
- Create a small experiment week—try one philosophy at a time and see what sparks joy.

Chapter 11: Finding Your Path

Now that you've seen the different philosophies, you can create a homeschool style that reflects your family. This is where freedom truly begins—the same freedom I celebrated in the introduction.

With so many options, how do you choose what's best?

Start by asking yourself some of these questions:

1. Why are you homeschooling?
   - Safety?
   - Health?
   - Academics?
   - Flexibility?
   - Faith?
2. What are your child's needs?
   - Do they crave structure?
   - Thrive with freedom?
   - Need extra support?
3. What are your strengths and limitations?
   If you have chronic illness, a flexible or online approach might fit best.
4. What season of life are you in?
   You can adjust as your family grows and changes.

Remember: This choice isn't permanent. You have full permission to tweak, experiment, and pivot.

🐝 Reflection | Prayer | Affirmation | Action

Choosing the Right Philosophy for Your Family

Reflection
1. What are the top three reasons you are homeschooling?
2. What is one non-negotiable you want to prioritize (faith, creativity, independence)?
3. How do you envision your homeschool day feeling?

Affirmation

I choose what serves my child's heart and mind—not what others expect.
Our homeschool path is valid, valuable, and uniquely ours.
I give myself permission to change, grow, and adapt along the way.

Prayer

Lord, Help me make choices rooted in wisdom, love, and peace—not fear or pressure.

Give me discernment as I consider what's best for our family's needs.

Let my heart stay open to learning and adjusting, knowing that this journey is not about perfection but purpose.

Thank You for reminding me that my way is enough. Amen.

Action
- Write down your top goals for your homeschool year.
- Choose a starting approach you want to try for 1–2 months.
- Plan a date to re-evaluate what's working.

Part II: Planning Your Homeschool

Chapter 12: Creating a Vision— What Matters Most?

When I first started homeschooling, I thought success depended on finding the right books, the right system, the right schedule. But over time, I realized what truly kept me steady wasn't the curriculum—it was the vision.

Your vision is your anchor. It reminds you why you started and what you hope your children will carry into adulthood. On the days when I was exhausted from sickle cell flare-ups or when life felt like too much, I could come back to our vision and breathe again.

Maybe your vision is about family time, faith, culture, creativity, or flexibility. There are no wrong answers. The important thing is to get clear on what matters most—so when doubt creeps in, you'll have something solid to hold onto.

A strong vision doesn't have to be long or polished. One or two heartfelt sentences are enough. For example:

1. Our homeschool is a safe, joyful space where learning is part of life.
2. We value curiosity, compassion, and growing together.

This isn't about sounding perfect—it's about knowing your "why." That purpose will guide your choices, set your pace, and bring peace when uncertainty rises.

🕊 Reflection | Prayer | Affirmation | Action

Creating a Vision

Reflection
1. What made you decide to homeschool in the first place?
2. What are the top three qualities you want your child to develop?
3. What do you want your homeschool days to feel like?

Affirmation
My homeschool vision is rooted in love, purpose, and what truly matters to us.
I am free to build a life of learning that reflects our values and dreams.
Our homeschool is not about perfection—it's about meaning.

Prayer
Dear God, Help me see beyond the daily tasks and into the heart of why we're doing this.

Show me the values You've planted in me and how to pass them on with intention.

Let our homeschool reflect what matters most—faith, connection, and joy.

Keep me grounded in our vision, especially when

challenges come. Amen.

Action Steps

- Write your homeschool vision statement in one or two sentences.
- Post it somewhere visible.
- Share your vision with your kids so they feel included.

Chapter 13: Setting Realistic Goals (Especially with Chronic Illness)

When I tried to homeschool like everyone else, I ended up in tears. I was comparing myself to healthy moms—moms with more money, energy, and time—while my reality looked completely different.

If you live with chronic illness—or just an unpredictable life—you need goals that honor your reality. Unrealistic expectations only create guilt and burnout. I learned that the hard way.

So instead of cramming too much into our days, I started setting flexible, gentle goals. I let our schedule flow naturally within a loose routine. Most days, I used a simple checklist and timeframe. As long as we completed the main goals of the day, we were successful.

When unexpected things happened (and they always did), I adjusted without shame. The program I use for core subjects includes a weekly student planner with daily assignments.

As long as I allowed time for those lessons, we stayed on track. That left space for our Bible study, life skills, and recreation—things that feed the soul, not just the mind.

Creating simple, achievable goals helped me build momentum over time without overwhelm. Start small and grow as you're able.

Examples of realistic goals:
- Complete math lessons 3–4 days per week, with room for breaks.
- Learn to cook three simple meals by the end of the year.
- Practice one calming strategy when feeling overwhelmed.

These goals honored where I was—not where I wished I could be. And that made all the difference.

🦋 Reflection | Prayer | Affirmation | Action

Setting Realistic Goals

Reflection
1. What does "realistic" look like for you right now?
2. Where have you been putting pressure on yourself to do more than you can?
3. What would it feel like to set goals that allow for grace?

Affirmation
I can set goals that honor my health, my family, and our current season.
I don't have to push past my limits to be a good teacher or mom.
Gentle, flexible progress is still progress.

Prayer
Lord, You know my body, my limits, and my heart.

Help me set goals that support my well-being while nurturing my children.

Teach me to rest without guilt and lead without fear.

May grace shape every plan and peace guide every step. Amen.

Action Steps

- Write one academic, one life skill, and one emotional goal.
- Circle the goal that feels most important.
- Brainstorm two to three small steps to move toward it.

Chapter 14: Choosing Curriculum — A Guide for the Overwhelmed

Picking curriculum can feel like walking into a giant warehouse where everything looks good—and everything costs too much. I can't tell you how many times I've ordered something only to realize it didn't fit our needs.

Over time, I learned to pause and ask myself a few simple questions before I clicked "buy":

- What's my budget? (I had to write mine down before shopping or I'd overspend.)
- How much structure do I want? (Am I piecing things together, or do I need open-and-go?)
- What format works best? (Books, online lessons, or a mix?)
- How independent is my child? (Can they work alone, or do they need my help?)
- How much energy do I have? (On tough days, can the curriculum keep going without me?)

The biggest lesson?

You don't need the perfect curriculum—you only need something good enough to start. You can always adjust later.

🕊 Reflection | Prayer | Affirmation | Action

Choosing Curriculum

Reflection
1. What has worked well for your child in the past?
2. What worries you most about choosing curriculum?
3. How do you define "enough" when it comes to academics?

Affirmation
I don't have to find the perfect curriculum—I just need one that works for us right now.
I trust my ability to choose wisely and adjust when needed.
My peace matters more than pressure.

Prayer
Dear God,
Help me make wise decisions with the resources I have.
Quiet the voices of fear and comparison.
Remind me that curriculum is a tool, not a test of my worth.
Guide me toward what will bless and serve my child and bring ease to our days. Amen.

Action
- Make a short list of two or three curriculum options.
- Read reviews or watch overview videos.
- Choose one to start with—knowing you can always pivot later.

Chapter 15: Creating a Flexible Schedule

When I worked night shifts and still had to homeschool during the day, I learned quickly: there is no one "right" schedule.

Some families do school in the mornings, others in the afternoons. Some learn year-round, while others take long seasonal breaks. For us, flexibility wasn't just helpful—it was survival.

Here are a few scheduling ideas that saved me:

- Four-Day Weeks: Leave one day open for appointments, errands, or rest.
- Loop Scheduling: Rotate subjects instead of stressing about missed days.
- Block Scheduling: Focus deeply on one subject at a time, then move to the next.

Our typical day looked like this:
- Breakfast and morning chores
- 2–3 learning activities
- Lunch and outdoor time
- Quiet time or creative projects

Not perfect. Not Pinterest. Just us—steady and flexible.

🕊 Reflection | Prayer | Affirmation | Action

Creating a Flexible Schedule

Reflection
1. What time of day do you and your child feel most focused?
2. What non-negotiables must be part of your routine?
3. What would a peaceful homeschool day look like?

Affirmation
Our homeschool rhythm is allowed to reflect our life, not fight against it.
I have the freedom to create a schedule that gives space for rest, growth, and joy.
Flexibility is not failure—it is wisdom.

Prayer
Lord, thank You for reminding me that our time is a gift.

Help me build routines that support peace, not pressure.

Guide me to create a schedule that honors our energy and capacity.

Let our days be anchored in grace and flow with intention. Amen.

Action

- Draft a sample weekly schedule.
- Highlight the parts you want to try first.
- Adjust after the first week based on what worked best.

Chapter 16: How to Track Progress (Without Burning Out)

In my early years of homeschooling, I tried to record everything—every worksheet, every page read, every assignment completed. That lasted about two weeks before I burned out.

Once, I even had to show records in court after my first ex took me to prove our eldest daughter was in school. The clerk looked completely overwhelmed by the stack of documentation I submitted. That day, I realized I had been doing more than enough. Then I learned the secret: simple is sustainable.

Depending on your state, you may need to keep attendance, samples of work, or progress reports. Even if it's not required, some tracking helps you appreciate how far your children have come.

Here are a few easy ways to track without stress:
- A binder with dividers for each subject
- Snapping photos of projects or experiments
- Keeping a simple notebook or digital log of what you did each day
- Printing a monthly calendar to mark attendance or key milestones

You don't need to document everything—just enough to show that learning is happening. And trust me, it is.

🐾 Reflection | Prayer | Affirmation | Action

How to Track Progress

Reflection
1. What kind of record-keeping feels realistic for you?
2. What helps you feel confident your child is learning?
3. What can you let go of?

Affirmation
I am capable of documenting our journey in simple, sustainable ways.
I don't need to prove everything—I can trust that learning is happening.
Our growth will speak for itself.

Prayer
Dear God,
Calm my anxious heart as I think about documentation and progress.

Help me focus on what truly matters, not on doing everything perfectly.

Give me creative, easy ways to record our learning with joy.

Let me celebrate small wins and release unnecessary burdens. Amen.

Action Steps

- Set up a folder or binder for each child.
- Decide on your tracking method (binder, app, or photos).
- Commit to updating records once a week or once a month.

Part III: Homeschooling with Chronic Illness

Chapter 17: You Matter Too: Self-Care for the Homeschooling Mom

It's easy to forget your needs when you're balancing teaching, parenting, and managing a chronic illness.

But hear this:
1. Your well-being is not optional.
2. You can't pour from an empty cup—and you don't have to.

Simple Self-Care Practices:
- Rest when you feel the warning signs of a flare.
- Keep a comfort basket (favorite snacks, meds, a heating pad) within reach.
- Make a list of low-energy activities your kids can do independently.
- Allow yourself to step back when needed—without guilt.

Self-care doesn't mean spa days (though those are lovely if you can).

It can look like:
- Saying no to extra commitments.
- Going to bed earlier.
- Drinking enough water.
- Asking for help.

Remember, you are a person first, and a

homeschooling mom second.

Once we remember that our needs matter, the next step is learning how to manage our limited energy. That's where Spoon Theory becomes such a powerful tool for homeschooling with chronic illness."

🌿 Reflection | Prayer | Affirmation | Action

You Matter Too: Self-Care for the Homeschooling Mom

Reflection
1. What signals does your body give you when you're reaching your limit?
2. What simple comforts help you feel cared for?
3. How do you talk to yourself on hard days?

Affirmation
I am worthy of care, rest, and compassion—just as much as my children.
Tending to my needs is not selfish; it is sacred.
When I care for myself, I teach my children to do the same.

Prayer
Dear Lord, Remind me that I am more than what I do.

Help me give myself permission to rest, to heal, and to receive.

Let me find peace in slowing down and grace in letting go.

When I feel worn out, fill me with Your comfort and

care. Amen.

Action

- Make a list of 3 self-care practices you can do this week.
- Create a "flare day kit" with supplies and activities.
- Schedule time to rest—even if it's only 10 minutes a day.

Chapter 18: Energy Management & Spoon Theory for Homeschoolers

If you've never heard of Spoon Theory, it's a way to explain how people with chronic illness budget their energy.

Imagine you start each day with a limited number of spoons. Each activity costs a spoon—sometimes more. When you run out, you can't just push through without consequences.

Homeschooling with limited spoons means planning carefully.

Tips for Energy Management:
- Prioritize must-do tasks.
- Alternate high-energy and low-energy activities.
- Take breaks before you feel depleted.
- Teach your kids to help with daily chores.
- If you have a big day planned, balance it with extra rest the day before and after.

Even with the best planning, some days will still be flare days. Let's talk about how to prepare for those hard days with grace and flexibility.

🦋 Reflection | Prayer | Affirmation | Action

Energy Management & Spoon Theory for Homeschoolers

Reflection
1. What activities drain you fastest?
2. What activities refill your energy?
3. How many "spoons" do you typically have each day?

Affirmation
My energy is valuable, and I have the right to manage it wisely.
I do not need to earn rest—I need to honor my limits.
I trust myself to create a rhythm that protects my well-being.

Prayer
God, You know every spoon I start with, and every task that takes from me.

Help me prioritize with wisdom and pace myself with patience.

Teach me to conserve energy without guilt and to value rest as holy work.

Thank You for walking with me through the ups and downs. Amen.

Action

- Write your top 3 daily energy-drainers and brainstorm ways to simplify or delegate them.
- Create a weekly plan with built-in rest days.
- Teach your kids about Spoon Theory so they understand your limits.

Chapter 19: Planning for Low-Energy or Flare Days

No matter how prepared you are, flare days happen.

Having a plan helps you avoid panic and guilt when they do.

Flare Day Strategies:
- Use independent learning tools (like online lessons or audiobooks).
- Keep a box of ready-to-go activities (puzzles, art supplies, educational shows).
- Focus on life skills—rest is learning too.
- Adjust expectations. Some days, surviving is enough.

Flare days remind us that we can't do this journey alone. Building a support system—whether in person or online—can make all the difference.

Important: You do not have to make up every missed lesson. Your homeschool is a marathon, not a sprint.

🕊 Reflection | Prayer | Affirmation | Action

Planning for Low-Energy or Flare Days

Reflection
1. What does a typical flare day look like for you?
2. What emotions come up when you can't do "enough"?
3. How can you remind yourself that rest has value?

Affirmation
Flare days do not define me—they remind me to slow down and listen.
Even when I can't do much, I am still enough.
Rest is not a setback; it's part of our homeschool rhythm.

Prayer
Lord, Give me strength on the days I have none.

Help me prepare with grace and respond with gentleness.

When guilt whispers, remind me that care is more powerful than perfection.

Let my children see love in my pauses and strength in my stillness. Amen.

Action

- Create a list of 5 independent activities your kids can do on flare days.
- Prepare a flare day basket with supplies.
- Write an encouraging note to yourself to read when you feel guilty.

Chapter 20: Building a Support System

You are not meant to do this alone.

Support doesn't always look like having a spouse who shares teaching or a family member who steps in. Sometimes it means leaning on a virtual community or hiring help where you can.

Types of Support:
- Emotional – Friends who listen without judgment.
- Practical – Relatives who watch the kids during appointments.
- Educational – Online co-ops or tutors.

If you don't have local support, look for:
- Facebook homeschool groups.
- Chronic illness communities.
- Local co-ops (some offer scholarships or sliding scale fees).

And as we lean on others, we also get to teach our children how to lean into life with resilience.

The way we model adaptability in our homeschool becomes one of the greatest lessons they'll ever learn.
Asking for help isn't weakness—it's wisdom.

🦋 Reflection | Prayer | Affirmation | Action

Building a Support System

Reflection Questions
1. Who in your life feels safe and supportive?
2. What kind of help would make the biggest difference?
3. How comfortable are you with asking for help?

Affirmation
I am not meant to carry this alone.
Asking for help is a sign of strength, not weakness.
Support is available to me, and I deserve to receive it.

Prayer
Dear God,
Surround me with safe people and soft places to land.

Open my heart to receive help without shame.

Guide me to the right communities and remind me that I'm not alone.

Help me speak my needs with confidence and find joy in shared burdens. Amen.

Action

- Make a list of 3 people you can ask for support.
- Join one online homeschool or chronic illness community this week.
- Create a "help wish list" so when someone offers, you know what to ask for.

Chapter 21: Teaching Your Kids While Teaching Resilience

One of the most powerful lessons you can teach your children is how to adapt when life is hard.

Your chronic illness isn't just an obstacle—it's an opportunity to model:
1. Patience
2. Self-advocacy
3. Compassion
4. Problem-solving

When you say, "I need to rest now," you teach them that all bodies deserve care. When you adapt plans, you teach flexibility.

Ideas to Involve Your Kids:
- Let them help plan the schedule.
- Assign age-appropriate chores.
- Share how you manage your health.
- Celebrate small wins together.

Your kids don't need perfection. They need your presence, your honesty, and your love.

🦬 Reflection | Prayer | Affirmation | Action

Your Kids While Teaching Resilience

Reflection
1. What do you hope your children learn from seeing you manage your health?
2. How do you talk to them about your illness?
3. What strengths have you seen in them already?

Affirmation
My children are learning strength, compassion, and adaptability through my journey.
I do not have to hide my struggles to be a good mother.
Our home is a place where real life teaches powerful lessons.

Prayer
Lord, Thank You for using even my hardest days to teach my children grace.

Help me be honest without fear, strong without hardness, and loving through it all.

Give me words to explain, and wisdom to model resilience.

Let my life be a quiet testimony of courage they'll carry forever. Amen.

Action Steps

- Plan a family conversation about your health (at an age-appropriate level).
- Make a chart of household tasks everyone can help with.
- Choose one way to celebrate resilience this month.

Part IV: Creating the Learning Environment

Chapter 22: Setting Up a Homeschool Space

(Tiny or Spacious)

You don't need a Pinterest-perfect classroom to homeschool successfully. I started at my dining room table.

Whether you have a dedicated room, a corner of your living room, or a kitchen table, what matters most is that your space feels welcoming, functional, and suited to your needs.

Tips for Creating a Homeschool Space:
1. Keep supplies accessible. Use rolling carts, bins, or baskets so you can tidy up easily.
2. Make it comfortable. Pillows, good lighting, and a cozy chair can make a big difference.
3. Display learning. Hang a small corkboard for artwork, goals, or visual reminders.
4. Rotate materials. Too much clutter can feel overwhelming. Keep out only what you need.

Homeschooling can happen anywhere: in bed, outside, or at the library. What matters most is that your environment supports peace, flexibility, and creativity.

Once your space feels supportive, the next challenge is teaching in that space—especially if you're juggling multiple ages or unique needs. Let's look at how to simplify that without losing your sanity.

🌿 Reflection | Prayer | Affirmation | Action

Setting Up a Homeschool Space

Reflection
1. What kind of space helps you and your kids feel calm?
2. What supplies do you use most often?
3. What's one thing you could remove to make your space feel better?

Affirmation
My homeschool space is enough.
I create an environment of peace, purpose, and joy—no matter the size.
Every corner of my home can hold learning and love.

Prayer
Lord, Thank You for the home You've given me.

Help me to see the beauty in what I already have and to create a learning space that reflects our needs and values.

Give me the creativity to make the most of small spaces and the wisdom to release perfection.

Let this space be filled with grace, growth, and goodness. Amen.

Action

- Choose a main area to be your "home base" for learning.
- Gather basic supplies into a single basket or shelf.
- Declutter one corner of your space this week.

Chapter 23: Homeschooling Multiple Ages or Special Needs

Teaching kids of different ages—or kids with special needs—can feel like juggling flaming swords. But with the right mindset and tools, you can make it manageable.

Strategies to Simplify:
- Use group learning: read-alouds, science experiments, and art can include everyone.
- Stagger start times: begin one child on independent work while teaching another.
- Adapt materials: adjust expectations and assignments by age and ability.
- Teach life skills: older kids can help younger siblings or assist with simple tasks.

If you have a child with special needs, remember:
1. Go at their pace.
2. Use accommodations.
3. Celebrate every small success.

You don't have to do it all at once. You just have to keep showing up.

Of course, we don't have to do this alone—technology can be a huge help when used wisely. From apps to online classes, let's explore tools that make homeschooling lighter, not heavier.

🦋 Reflection | Prayer | Affirmation | Action

Homeschooling Multiple Ages or Special Needs

Reflection
1. What is your biggest challenge with teaching multiple ages or abilities?
2. What has worked well so far?
3. What can you simplify or combine?

Affirmation
I am capable of teaching each of my children in the way they learn best.
I trust my instincts, adapt with love, and embrace progress over perfection.
My home is a space of inclusion, patience, and purpose.

Prayer
God, Thank You for the beautiful variety in my children.

When the days feel complicated and I doubt my ability, remind me that You have equipped me to meet each child where they are.

Give me grace to be flexible, strength to stay steady, and joy in the small victories.

Help me celebrate every step forward, no matter how small. Amen.

Action

- Make a list of activities everyone can do together.
- Create independent work bins for each child.
- Plan one group lesson this week.

Chapter 24: Tech Tools, Apps, and Resources

Technology can be your best friend—especially when you need a break or extra support.

Helpful Tech Tools:
1. Time4Learning – Online curriculum covering core subjects
2. Khan Academy – Free video lessons for all grade levels
3. Outschool – Affordable live classes on almost any topic
4. Epic! – Huge library of e-books and audiobooks for kids
5. Duolingo – Language learning app
6. YouTube – Tutorials and documentaries (always preview content first)

Tech Boundaries:
- Set limits on screen time.
- Use parental controls.
- Balance tech with hands-on learning.

But homeschooling isn't only about academics and apps. Life skills, hobbies, and rest are just as valuable—and often the things our kids remember most. Let's talk about how to weave those into your days.

🦋 Reflection | Prayer | Affirmation | Action

Tech Tools, Apps, and Resources

Reflection
1. What role do you want technology to play in your homeschool?
2. Which apps or platforms have you tried and liked?
3. What concerns do you have about tech use?

Affirmation
I use technology with purpose and wisdom.
I choose resources that support my child's growth and protect their peace.
I am guided, not overwhelmed, by the tools available to me.

Prayer
Dear Lord, Thank You for the tools that make learning more accessible and flexible.

Help me discern what aligns with our values and learning goals.

Guard our hearts and minds from distractions and lead us to the right resources at the right time.

Help me use technology as a tool—not a replacement—for connection, creativity, and curiosity. Amen.

Action

- Pick one new tech resource to explore.
- Decide on daily or weekly screen time guidelines.
- Bookmark your favorite websites for quick access.

Chapter 25: Incorporating Life Skills, Hobbies, and Rest

Homeschooling isn't just about academics. Life skills, hobbies, and rest are just as valuable.

In fact, they're essential for raising resilient, capable kids.

Ideas for Life Skills:
- Cooking and meal planning
- Budgeting and saving money
- Basic cleaning and laundry
- Time management

Hobbies to Explore:
- Gardening
- Drawing or painting
- Coding
- Music

Rest Matters:
- Schedule downtime.
- Take nature breaks.
- Allow free play.

When you build these into your homeschool, you teach your children that a good life is about more than checking boxes—it's about wholeness.

As we weave life into learning, we also recognize that homeschooling happens alongside everything else in our lives—including our health. Some days we're not just the teacher, but also the nurse, the patient, and the mom holding it all together. Let's talk about blending those roles with grace.

🦋 Reflection | Prayer | Affirmation | Action

Incorporating Life Skills, Hobbies, and Rest

Reflection Questions
1. What life skills do you most want your kids to learn?
2. What hobbies light them up?
3. How can you make rest a priority in your week?

Affirmation
I am raising whole, wise, and well-balanced children. Our homeschool includes joy, rest, curiosity, and care. There is beauty and purpose in every part of our rhythm.

Prayer
God, Thank You for reminding me that learning is more than textbooks.

Help me value the soft skills—the laughter in the kitchen, the joy in a paintbrush, the peace in a pause.

Give me clarity to build routines that nourish our souls, not just fill our time.

Bless our home with balance, rest, and renewal. Amen.

Action

- Pick one life skill to focus on this month.
- Plan a weekly time for hobbies or creative projects.
- Schedule a rest day (or afternoon) each week.

Part V: Teaching Strategies for Real Life

Chapter 26: When You're the Teacher and the Nurse: Combining Roles

When you're homeschooling while managing your health, you wear many hats—educator, nurse, mom, and motivator—all before noon.

It's a lot. But you don't have to choose one role over the other. You can blend them with grace, creativity, and preparation.

Tips for Combining Roles:
1. Honor your limits. When you're not feeling well, it's okay to scale back to the essentials.
2. Use independent learning time. While you rest or tend to your health, your child can read, watch educational videos, or work through simple tasks.
3. Be transparent. Honest, age-appropriate conversations about your health teach empathy and compassion.
4. Plan ahead. Keep a "Plan B" folder of low-prep activities for days when you need extra rest.

Of course, being both teacher and nurse reminds us that homeschooling doesn't always need to look traditional. Sometimes the most meaningful learning happens outside of a textbook—through creativity, projects, and hands-on experiences."

Reflection | Prayer | Affirmation | Action

When You're the Teacher and the Nurse: Combining Roles

Reflection
1. What are your biggest challenges in balancing your health and homeschooling?
2. What do you hope your children learn about rest, resilience, and self-care by watching you?
3. How can you remind yourself that doing your best is enough?

Affirmation
I am doing enough, even on the slow days.
My children are learning strength, adaptability, and love through the way I care for myself and for them.

Prayer
Lord, Thank You for sustaining me in this season.

Help me to honor my body while still showing up for my children.

Teach me to release guilt and replace it with grace. When I feel weak, remind me that rest is sacred.

Let my children see not only what I teach—but the love, faith, and endurance behind it. Amen.

Action

- Create a list of go-to lessons for low-energy days.
- Write a script you can use to explain when you need a break.
- Identify one small way you can ask for or accept help.

Chapter 27: Teaching Without a Textbook: Creative, Hands-On, or Project-Based Learning

Not everything has to come from a workbook. In fact, some of the most powerful learning happens when kids get messy, curious, and creative.

Ideas for Hands-On Learning:
- Science experiments with kitchen supplies
- Gardening and nature observation
- Building models with blocks or recycled items
- Cooking and baking as math and science
- History through storytelling, documentaries, or art

Project-Based Learning:
- Let your child dive into a topic they love. Research it. Create something. Share what they've learned.

Project Examples:
- Build a diorama of a favorite animal habitat
- Make a family recipe book
- Design a board game based on a book or subject
- Interview grandparents and create a family history timeline

When we let go of rigid methods, it's only natural to also let go of rigid schedules.

Homeschooling allows us to embrace flexibility—shaping our days and years in ways that fit our family's health, energy, and lifestyle.

🕊 Reflection | Prayer | Affirmation | Action

Teaching Without a Textbook: Creative, Hands-On, or Project-Based Learning

Reflection
1. What sparks your child's curiosity most?
2. Are there ways to combine creativity with learning goals?
3. What project could your child start (or finish) this month?

Affirmation
Learning happens through play, creation, and exploration.
I trust that joy, wonder, and imagination are just as important as books and grades.

Prayer
God, Thank You for giving my children curious minds and creative spirits.

Help me nurture their natural talents without fear or pressure.

Show me how to guide them gently, celebrate their ideas, and make space for fun.

Let our homeschool be a place where learning is joyful and alive. Amen.

Action
- Brainstorm 2–3 project ideas with your child.
- Gather materials for one hands-on lesson.
- Block out a day this week for creative learning.

Chapter 28: Embracing Educational Flexibility

One of the best things about homeschooling? You get to write your own calendar.

You're not bound to public school timelines. You can adjust your schedule to reflect your family's rhythm, needs, and lifestyle.

Flexible Schedule Options:
1. Year-Round Homeschooling: Spread learning across 12 months with regular breaks.
2. 4-Day Weeks: Reserve one day for rest, field trips, or catch-up.
3. Block Scheduling: Focus deeply on one subject for a few weeks at a time.
4. Time-of-Day Flexibility: Some kids thrive in the morning; others learn better in the evening.

Try it. Adjust it.
Make it your own.

And just as we have freedom with schedules, we also have freedom with teaching. We don't have to carry every subject on our own shoulders.

Outsourcing certain lessons or leaning on community can lighten our load and enrich our children's education.

🦬 Reflection | Prayer | Affirmation | Action

Embracing Educational Flexibility

Reflection
1. What kind of weekly rhythm supports your family's mental and physical health?
2. When are your kids most alert and focused?
3. How would it feel to let go of traditional rules and honor your family's natural flow?

Affirmation
We are free to learn in ways that fit us.
Our rhythm is sacred. Our homeschool reflects our real life—not a system we don't belong to.

Prayer
Dear God, Thank You for the freedom to educate my children in a way that works for us.

Help me tune into our unique pace and needs without comparing our journey to anyone else's.

Give me the confidence to break from tradition when it brings more peace and purpose.

Help me create a flow that honors our energy, values, and well-being. Amen.

Action

- Choose one scheduling change you'd like to try.
- Test it out for a month.
- Keep what works, and release what doesn't—with no guilt.

Chapter 29: Outsourcing Subjects

Mama, you don't have to teach everything.

You are not a failure for needing support—you are wise for seeking it.

Benefits of Outsourcing:
- Reduces your workload and stress
- Allows your child to learn from others
- Provides variety and community
- Gives you time to rest or handle other responsibilities

Ways to Outsource:
- Online Classes: Platforms like Outschool, Khan Academy, or local virtual academies
- Co-ops: Join a group that shares teaching responsibilities
- Tutors: In-person or online for tough subjects
- Family Help: Let a trusted relative teach a skill or subject they love

Start small.

One class.

One subject.

One semester at a time.

🦋 Reflection | Prayer | Affirmation | Action

Outsourcing Subjects

Reflection
1. Which subjects or tasks drain you the most?
2. Who or what could support you in that area?
3. What would change in your life if you accepted help?

Affirmation
I don't have to do it all to be a great homeschool mom.
Letting others help my child grow is an act of wisdom, not weakness.

Prayer
Lord, Thank You for the helpers, teachers, and resources You place in our path.

Help me release the pressure to do everything alone.

Give me discernment about where to seek help and who to trust.

Let my children flourish through the village You are building around us. Amen.

Action
- Research one outsourcing option.
- Talk to your child about what they'd like to learn with someone else.
- Make a plan to try outsourcing one subject this semester.

Part VI: Socialization & Emotional Health

Chapter 30: Helping Kids Make Friends (Even If You're Mostly Home)

I've always had a house full of kids—nieces, nephews, neighbors, friends—so my children were never short on socializing.

One of the most overlooked places for meeting new friends is the local park. I make sure my kids go out to play a few times a day, especially when I know other neighborhood kids are outside.

This simple rhythm allows friendships to grow naturally.

Our family has truly been blessed by God. When new neighbors moved in next door, they turned out to be amazing—the kids were all similar ages, and everyone clicked right away.

Before long, my house became the hangout spot, and I had the joy of watching friendships blossom right under my roof.

Over the years, my kids have been surrounded by friends and family who've felt like extended family. Cousins have stayed with us for days or even weeks at a time.

It's been such a joy watching how my children respond to conflict, show empathy, and navigate moral situations.

But let's be clear—just because your children are homeschooled and raised a certain way doesn't mean they won't encounter kids with different values or backgrounds.

That's why character building is so important. The goal isn't to shield them from every challenge but to equip them with strong moral foundations so they can adapt, choose good company, and cultivate lasting, healthy friendships.

🐝 Reflection | Prayer | Affirmation | Action

Helping Kids Make Friends

Reflection
1. How can I create more opportunities for my child to connect with peers?
2. Do I encourage social time as much as I encourage academics?

Affirmation
I trust that the right connections will come at the right time.
My child is growing in love, confidence, and community—one step at a time.

Prayer
God, help me create opportunities for meaningful friendships for my child.
Lead us to safe, nurturing spaces where we can both feel seen and supported.
Teach us to be open, brave, and kind in new relationships. Amen.

Action
- This week, plan one intentional opportunity for socialization—visit a park, library event, church group, or invite a neighbor over.
- Notice how your child responds, and celebrate their courage in connecting with others.

Chapter 31: Handling Criticism and Doubts from Others

When I first started homeschooling, I faced a lot of judgment. I didn't know anyone else doing it—I was literally the first in my circle.

Some family members made me feel inadequate. They would quiz my kids, as if homeschooling meant they had to be geniuses. I'd get questions about my competency: "Don't you need a degree? Shouldn't you be a teacher?"

But I'm thankful I didn't listen to those doubts or give up. My children are now some of the smartest, kindest, and most respectful kids people know.

Those same critics now ask me how I do it—and honestly, that's part of what inspired me to write this book. God truly has a way of turning our tests into testimonies and our shortcomings into blessings for others.

If you're feeling the sting of criticism, keep going. Keep following what God placed in your heart. Who knows your children better than you? And remember—if you don't want your kids to end up like theirs, maybe you shouldn't be listening to their opinions in the first place.

🐝 Reflection | Prayer | Affirmation | Action

Handling Criticism and Doubts from Others

Reflection
1. Whose opinions about homeschooling matter most to me?
2. Am I allowing criticism to plant seeds of doubt where God has already given me clarity?

Affirmation
I don't need to explain or defend what God has called me to do.
I am equipped, empowered, and enough for this journey.

Prayer
Lord, give me strength when I feel misunderstood and peace when others question my path.

Help me stay rooted in truth, not fear.

Let my confidence be a testimony of Your guidance. Amen.

Action
The next time criticism comes, respond with peace instead of defense.
Simply say, "This is what works for our family," and move forward without guilt.

Chapter 32: Supporting Your Child's Mental Health & Emotions

I have four children—three daughters and one son—but in reality, any given week feels like managing twenty different personalities and emotions.

Each child is learning how to regulate feelings while also processing life experiences—grief, change, or disappointment. Our family has walked through death, divorce, depression, and disability.

I do my best to create a home where everyone feels safe to share their thoughts and emotions. Does it always go perfectly? Not at all. But my goal is to stay open, listen, and be honest.

My son, for example, sometimes struggles to find words for his feelings. When he gets overwhelmed, I give him all the time he needs to speak without interruption. If I see him really stuck, I'll gently help when I see struggle—but most of the time, I let him finish his thought on his own. That sense of control empowers him.

Another thing I do is help name emotions. Once he works through a wave of feelings, I explain what he might be experiencing and remind him that all feelings are valid—but our actions still need to stay under control.

With my daughters, our conversations have grown deeper—about womanhood, identity, and relationships.

Still, I want them to know they can show up as their full selves without shame or fear.

Building that kind of bond takes time, but it's worth it. Our relationships with our children are some of the most sacred gifts we'll ever receive.

❧ Reflection | Prayer | Affirmation | Action

Supporting Your Child's Mental Health & Emotions

Reflection
1. How do I usually respond when my child expresses big emotions?
2. Do I listen first, or do I rush to fix, dismiss, or control?

Affirmation
I am creating a safe space where my child feels heard, valued, and emotionally supported.
We are learning and healing together.

Prayer
God, grant me patience and wisdom as I walk beside my child in their emotional journey.
Show me how to love deeply, listen fully, and guide gently.
Help us grow stronger through compassion and connection. Amen.

Action
Set aside one intentional "emotion check-in" this week.
Ask your child how they're feeling. Listen without correcting, and reflect their words back:
"I hear you saying you feel ____. That makes sense."

Chapter 33: Celebrating Progress Without Comparison

When I first started homeschooling, my ex would always talk about child prodigies—kids graduating college at thirteen as neuroscientists. I'd read about other homeschooling moms who seemed to have it all together. Meanwhile, I was relearning lessons just to teach them the next day and feeling like I was failing.

Then one day, I looked at my children and realized: I needed to build our homeschool around them, not around someone else's story. My kids were different ages, with unique learning styles and needs. Of course it felt chaotic—I was trying to recreate public school at home or copy someone else's plan.

When I shifted to doing things our way, everything changed. We began celebrating our own wins, based on our own goals.

If our goal for the week was to spell and write a full name, and we only made it through the first name, we still celebrated—with popsicles. When the full name was mastered, we celebrated again—with ice cream cones.

Those small celebrations reminded me that progress is progress. Comparison truly is the thief of joy, and when you let it go, peace follows.

🦬 Reflection | Prayer | Affirmation | Action

Celebrating Progress Without Comparison

Reflection
Am I measuring my child's growth by someone else's standards—or am I honoring their unique pace and progress?

Affirmation
I release the need to compare.
My journey is valid. My child's progress is worthy of celebration—just as it is.

Prayer
Lord, help me see the beauty in our unique path.

Let gratitude silence comparison.

Teach me to rejoice in every small win and trust that

You are working in every moment—even the slow ones. Amen.

Action
This week, choose one milestone your child has reached—big or small—and celebrate it.
Write it down, take a photo, or add it to a "victory jar" as a reminder of God's faithfulness in your homeschool journey.

Part VII: Navigating Hard Days & Burnout

Chapter 34: Recognizing Burnout Early

When I first started homeschooling, I was a stay-at-home mom. Later, when I went back to work, I hid the fact that I was burned out. I wanted everything to look fine on the outside, even though I was struggling. For financial stability, I didn't think I could stay home.

But working full-time midnights, homeschooling during the day, and maintaining a home would be enough to burn out any momma. Add sickle cell anemia, and I was playing a dangerous game with my health.

Now I've learned the power of using a planner and pacing myself—and my children. Burnout doesn't just happen to moms; kids get burned out too. If they have too much of one thing, they lose interest and become frustrated.

That's why breaks matter for everyone. Switching up activities, mixing learning methods, and allowing time to rest keeps the day flowing. And when my kids finish their schoolwork, I don't pile on extra just to fill the hours. Done is done. (That doesn't mean early access to gaming or social media—it just means free play, creativity, or rest.)

The key is pacing yourself, and pacing your children.

🕊 Reflection | Prayer | Affirmation | Action

Recognizing Burnout Early

Reflection
1. What are the early warning signs that I—or my child—may be burning out?
2. How can I build more rest and variety into our homeschool rhythm?

Affirmation
I honor my limits without shame. Rest is not weakness—it is wisdom. I am worthy of care, too.

Prayer
Lord, help me recognize the quiet signs when I'm running on empty.
Remind me that I am not a machine, but a human being in need of grace.
Let me rest without guilt, and refuel in Your presence.
Teach me to be gentle with myself. Amen

Action
This week, schedule one intentional break for yourself and one for your children. Treat it as just as important as a lesson plan.

Chapter 35: Simple Plans for Hard Weeks

I have plans for the easy days and the hard ones. My kids already know our regular routine, but I also keep a few "secret plans" tucked away just for me.

Because my health fluctuates, our schedule can change in an instant. So I would plan fun extras—field trips, nature walks, beach days, or science projects—without telling them ahead of time. That way, if I had to cancel due to my health or budget, my kids weren't disappointed.

Sometimes, those backup plans were as simple as an "educational movie day" or pulling out an easy workbook. It wasn't failure—it was flexibility. Having these simple alternatives made even the hardest weeks manageable.

🦬 Reflection | Prayer | Affirmation | Action

Simple Plans for Hard Weeks

Reflection
What backup activities or lessons can I keep ready for the days when life feels too heavy?

Affirmation
Even on hard days, I am doing enough. I don't need perfection—just presence, patience, and peace.

Prayer
God, walk with me through the chaos and the crisis.

When life feels like too much, help me simplify without shame.

Show me how to lead my children with love, even when my energy is low.

Fill our home with peace, even in the storm. Amen

Action
Create a "hard week" box with simple resources—workbooks, educational games, documentaries, or art supplies. Keep it ready for when you need it.

Chapter 36: Grace Over Guilt: You Are Enough

During our homeschooling journey, our family has faced highs and lows.

There were seasons I felt I wasn't doing enough for my children's education. My health needs were so overwhelming that lessons sometimes had to be set aside. Some days, my kids slacked, and I was too drained to correct them.

But prayer carried me. I knew in my heart the plans I had for my children, and I knew no one else would care as deeply as I did. Even when I felt like I was failing, my love for them never wavered.

Eventually, I learned to forgive myself. As a mom, I gave myself grace. As their teacher, I made better plans and built more structure. Both were acts of love.

As moms sometimes we are our toughest critics. Let us learn to give ourselves the grace and space we know we deserve.

🦬 Reflection | Prayer | Affirmation | Action

Grace Over Guilt: You Are Enough

Reflection
1. Where am I carrying guilt in my homeschooling journey?
2. How might God be inviting me to replace it with grace?

Affirmation
I am enough. What I give—imperfect, messy, beautiful—is exactly what my children need today.

Prayer
Dear God, release me from the weight of guilt.
Help me to see myself through Your eyes—loved, chosen, enough.
Teach me to offer myself the same compassion I give to others.
Let grace be louder than shame. Amen

Action
Write down three ways you've shown up for your children this week. Thank God for each one, no matter how small.

Chapter 37: Emergency Plans for Flare-Ups or Hospitalizations

With chronic illness and homeschooling, it's best to stay ready. That's why I use Time4Learning as our core curriculum—it has been life-changing.

The program tracks assignments and provides student planners, so my kids know exactly what's expected of them. They don't have to wait for me to explain; they log in, see their lessons, and get to work.

I also keep grade-level workbooks on hand, especially for times when my children may need to spend the day with family. Workbooks are easy to use for both the child and the temporary caregiver.

The biggest gift you can give your child—and yourself—is good record-keeping.

Keeping track of their progress ensures that if anything ever happens to you, others will know where they are in their learning. It also provides what's needed if your child has to be enrolled in school unexpectedly.

❧ Reflection | Prayer | Affirmation | Action

Emergency Plans for Flare-Ups or Hospitalizations

Reflection
1. If I had an emergency today, would my child's education stay on track?
2. What can I put in place now to ease that burden later?

Affirmation
I am doing what I can to prepare, not from fear, but from love. My strength is in my planning—and in my surrender.

Prayer
Lord, in the face of uncertainty, give me peace.
Help me build a plan that brings stability and calm, even in crisis.
Be with my children when I cannot, and surround us with the support we need.
You are our safety, our provider, our rock. Amen

Action
Take one step this week to strengthen your emergency plan—set up a binder with lesson records, prepare a caregiver's guide, or organize backup materials.

Part VIII: Long-Term Homeschooling

Graduating, Letting Go & Moving Forward.

Chapter 38: Reevaluating Each Year: Stay, Pause, or Pivot?

Homeschooling isn't a decision you make once and never revisit. Every year—sometimes every season—

I had to ask myself hard questions:
- Is this still working for us?
- Do my kids need a change?
- Am I still able to show up in a healthy way?

There were years when I kept going strong, and there were years when I was barely holding it together. I learned that stopping to reevaluate didn't mean I was quitting—it meant I cared enough to pay attention.

When I gave myself permission to pause or pivot, it actually freed me. I realized this is a path, not a prison. Some seasons looked like full schedules with planners and unit studies. Other seasons looked like survival mode—documentaries, library books, and grace.

And you know what? My kids learned in both.

Reflection | Prayer | Affirmation | Action

Reevaluating Each Year: Stay, Pause, or Pivot?

Reflection
1. What has worked best about homeschooling so far?
2. What has been hardest?
3. What might you want to change in the next season?

Affirmation
Every season brings new clarity. I trust myself to make the best decision for this chapter of our lives.

Prayer
Lord, give me discernment as I reflect on where we've been and where we're going. Quiet the noise of fear or pressure and help me hear Your voice. Teach me to pivot without shame and rest when needed. Thank You for walking with us through every season. Amen

Action
- Set aside time annually to review your homeschool goals.
- Make a "pros and cons" list about continuing vs. other options.
- Pray or journal about any big decisions ahead.

Chapter 39: High School at Home: Transcripts, Credits, & Graduation

Whew—high school. I'll be honest, this one scared me the most. I kept wondering: Can I really prepare my kids for life after high school?

But once I broke it down, I realized it's less about perfection and more about record-keeping and guidance.

Here's what I learned:
- Transcripts matter, but they're not as scary as they sound. I kept a simple spreadsheet of courses, grades, and credits.
- Credits are usually around 20–24 to graduate, but you can check your state's requirements.
- Testing like the SAT/ACT is optional for some paths but helpful for others.
- Diplomas—yes, you can issue one as a homeschool parent. And your child can walk proudly into whatever future they choose.

I reminded myself often: my role was not to have every answer, but to guide, pray, and prepare my child with love.

Reflection | Prayer | Affirmation | Action
High School at Home: Transcripts, Credits, & Graduation

Reflection
1. What are your child's goals after high school?
2. How comfortable are you with planning high school credits?
3. What help might you need to feel confident?

Affirmation
I am capable of guiding my child through high school with wisdom and care. We are learning, growing, and preparing for greatness.

Prayer
God, give me peace as we step into this new chapter. Help me organize, prepare, and walk beside my child with confidence.
Remind me that I don't have to have all the answers—just a willing heart and Your steady hand to lead us. Amen

Action
- Download a transcript template.
- Research your state's graduation requirements.
- Talk to your teen about their interests and plans.

Chapter 40: College, Trade School, or Alternative Paths

When my kids started dreaming about life after high school, I had to wrestle with my own expectations.

I grew up thinking college was the only "right" path. But life—and chronic illness—taught me that success comes in many forms.

Some of my kids leaned toward college. Others were curious about trades or creative paths.

I learned to celebrate all of it. Because what matters most isn't prestige—it's purpose.

Whether your child chooses a 4-year degree, community college, trade school, entrepreneurship, or even a gap year, know this:

you've already equipped them with resilience and resourcefulness by homeschooling.

That's a gift no diploma can measure.

Reflection | Prayer | Affirmation | Action

College, Trade School, or Alternative Paths

Reflection
1. What dreams does your child have for their future?
2. What practical steps can you take to support them?
3. How can you celebrate all paths equally?

Affirmation
My child's future is full of promise. I celebrate the path that's right for them—not what the world expects, but what aligns with their purpose.

Prayer
Lord, help me release control and embrace Your plan for my child's future.
Guide them to meaningful work, calling, and joy. Whether they go to college, learn a trade, or start a business, remind us that all purpose-driven paths are valid in Your eyes.

Action
- Schedule a conversation about future plans.
- Research scholarships and financial aid resources.
- Make a list of colleges, training programs, or jobs that interest your child.

Chapter 41: What If I Can't Continue? Planning for Transition

This chapter is close to my heart. There were times when my health had me asking, what if I can't keep going?

As moms, we want to believe we can push through anything. But the truth is, sometimes life shifts—illness, finances, family changes. If you need to stop homeschooling, it doesn't mean you failed. It means you adapted.

I made sure to keep good records, not just for legal reasons, but so if my children needed to transition into public or private school, there would be no confusion.

I also had honest conversations with them: that homeschooling was a blessing, but it wasn't the only way to be educated.

This was one of the hardest lessons to learn: letting go can be love, too.

🕊 Reflection | Prayer | Affirmation | Action

What If I Can't Continue? Planning for Transition

Reflection
1. What fears do you have about ending homeschooling?
2. What would you need to feel at peace with a transition?
3. How can you honor all you've accomplished?

Affirmation
Letting go is not failure—it's wisdom, love, and strength. I can honor what we built and still move forward.

Prayer
God, meet me in the fear and the unknown.
If I need to change direction, help me do so with grace.
Remind me that what I've poured into my children will never be wasted.
Wrap me in peace and remind me:

I did my best, and You'll take it from here. Amen

Action
- Create a folder with your homeschool records.
- Identify schools you could transition to if needed.
  - Write yourself a letter of encouragement, reminding yourself that you did your best.

Part IX: Inspiration & Resources

Chapter 42: Real Moms' Stories: Homeschooling Through Illness

Sometimes, you just need to hear: "Me too."

In this chapter, you'll read short stories and quotes from mothers who have homeschooled while navigating chronic illness, disabilities, and overwhelming seasons.
Their journeys remind us that even when the days are hard, we are not alone.

Story Snippets:
"I have lupus and used to think homeschooling was impossible. But by creating a four-day week and letting go of perfection, I found our groove. My daughter is thriving."

"During chemo treatments, my boys did most of their lessons online. When I felt up to it, we read books together. We still look back on that year with gratitude for the time we had."

"I live with severe fatigue. Our homeschool is built around my energy patterns. Mornings are our learning time; afternoons are for rest and creative play."

You are not alone. Others have walked this road—and they are cheering for you.

🦋 Reflection | Prayer | Affirmation | Action
Real Moms' Stories: Homeschooling Through Illness

Reflection
1. Which stories resonate with you?
2. What do you wish other people understood about homeschooling with illness?
3. What strengths have you discovered in yourself?

Affirmation
I am not alone. My story matters, and my journey inspires others.

Prayer
Lord, thank You for the community of moms who walk this path alongside me.
When I feel weary or isolated, remind me of their strength and hope.
Help me to see my own courage and to offer grace to myself each day. Amen.

Action
- Write your own homeschool story—just a page for yourself.
- Reach out to an online community or friend for encouragement.
- Save a favorite quote to read when you feel alone.

Chapter 43: Favorite Curricula by Energy Level

Some days, we are thriving. Some days, we are just surviving.

Here are curriculum ideas to match your energy, so you can keep learning flowing without guilt.

Low-Energy Days:
- Time4Learning (online, self-paced)
- Teaching Textbooks (math)
- Epic! (audiobooks & e-books)
- Documentaries (Curiosity Stream, PBS)

Medium-Energy Days:
- The Good and the Beautiful (open-and-go lessons)
- Easy lapbooks or unit studies
- Short science experiments

High-Energy Days:
- Project-based learning
- Nature walks and field trips
- Art or cooking projects

🦋 Reflection | Prayer | Affirmation | Action

Favorite Curricula by Energy Level

Reflection
1. What kind of curriculum has worked best for your family?
2. How do your energy levels typically fluctuate?
3. What resources could you add or drop to make life easier?

Affirmation
I honor my energy and adapt my teaching with grace. Every day looks different—and that's okay.

Prayer
God, guide me in choosing tools and resources that support our unique rhythm.
Help me to be gentle with myself when energy runs low, trusting that each step forward is progress.
Amen

Action
- Make a list of go-to activities for low, medium, and high-energy days.
- Evaluate your current curriculum—does it still serve you?
- Choose one new resource to try this season.

Chapter 44: Books, Podcasts, and Online Communities

You don't have to figure this out alone. Inspiration, ideas, and encouragement are just a click—or a page—away.

Books:
- The Brave Learner by Julie Bogart
- Teaching from Rest by Sarah Mackenzie
- The Read-Aloud Family by Sarah Mackenzie

Podcasts:
- The Homeschool Sisters Podcast
- Your Morning Basket
- Raising Lifelong Learners
- The Warrior Mom Guides Podcast (coming soon)

Online Communities:
- Facebook: Homeschooling with Chronic Illness
- Instagram: #homeschoollife #homeschoolmom
- Local co-op Facebook groups

🦋 Reflection | Prayer | Affirmation | Action

Books, Podcasts, and Online Communities

Reflection
1. What books or podcasts inspire you most?
2. Where could you connect with like-minded families?
3. How can you build community without draining your energy?

Affirmation
I am part of a supportive community that uplifts and encourages me.

Prayer
Lord, thank You for the connections and resources You provide.
Help me to find and nurture relationships that refresh my spirit and encourage my family. Amen

Action
- Pick one podcast to try this week.
- Join an online group or follow an inspiring account.
- Share something about your journey with a community.

Chapter 45: Printable Templates: Planners, Checklists, Daily Logs

Find tools that fit your life make homeschooling more peaceful and sustainable.

Some tools I have in my toolkit includes the following:
- Weekly Lesson Plan
- Attendance Log
- Reading List
- Progress Tracker
- Daily Schedule
- Unit Study Planner

Visit the warrior mom academy book shop for more tools and Homeschool HelpHers™.

Reflection | Prayer | Affirmation | Action

Printable Templates: Planners, Checklists, Daily Logs

Reflection
1. Which printable tools would help you feel organized?
2. Do you prefer paper or digital planning?
3. What can you delegate or simplify?

Affirmation
I am organized in a way that supports peace and progress in our homeschool.

Prayer
God, grant me clarity and calm as I plan our days. Help me to use my time wisely and to release what no longer serves us. Amen

Action
- Print or customize one planning template.
- Set aside time weekly to review and adjust your plans.
- Keep your templates somewhere easy to access.

You Were Made for This
(Even If It Doesn't Feel Like It)

Mama,
I know this feels big—because it is. Homeschooling is one of the bravest, most loving choices you can make.

You won't do it perfectly.
You will have days when you want to quit.
You will wonder if you're failing your kids.

But you are enough. Your kids don't need perfect—they need you. They need your courage, your faith, your laughter, your imperfect love. And no curriculum can ever replace that.

Take this journey one day at a time, one moment at a time. Keep showing up—and remember: you were made for this. I'm so proud of you.

Affirmation
I am enough just as I am. My love and presence are the greatest gifts I give my children.

Prayer
Lord, when I feel overwhelmed or uncertain, remind me that I am Your beloved child, equipped with everything I need. Strengthen my heart and renew my spirit. Help me to trust the journey and embrace each imperfect moment with grace. Amen.

Encouragement for the Journey Ahead

Homeschooling is not a sprint; it's a lifelong adventure filled with lessons for both you and your children.

As you move forward:
- Celebrate small victories. Even a single successful read-aloud or a hands-on project completed is progress.
- Give yourself grace. Some days will be messy—and that's okay. Your presence matters more than perfection.
- Build community. Lean on other homeschooling families, mentors, and local or online support groups.
- Trust your instincts. You know your child best, even when the world doubts your choices.
- Remember your why. Your children are learning not just academics—they're learning resilience, faith, and love.

Every challenge is an opportunity.

Every low-energy day is a chance to model perseverance.

You are not just teaching subjects—you are teaching life.

Scriptures for Teaching & Patience

Proverbs 22:6 (NLT)
Train children in the right way, and when old, they will not stray.

Deuteronomy 6:6-7 (NIV)
These commandments that I give you today are to be on your hearts. Impress them on your children.

James 1:19 (NLT)
Everyone should be quick to listen, slow to speak, and slow to become angry.

Colossians 3:21 (NLT)
Fathers, do not embitter your children, or they will become discouraged.

Closing Prayer:
Lord, give me patience, wisdom, and creativity as I teach and guide my children. Help me nurture them in love and faith.

Book Club & Reflection Questions

Use these questions for personal reflection, discussion with a partner, or a homeschooling book club:

1. What fears or doubts do you have about homeschooling, and where do they come from?
2. What do you want your children to remember most about learning at home with you?
3. How does your health or life situation affect your confidence to homeschool—and how can you plan for support?
4. What would a "successful" homeschool year look like for your family, not by someone else's standards?
5. If you had no judgment or pressure, how would you ideally want your child to learn?
6. How can you celebrate your wins, no matter how small, and let go of unnecessary guilt?
7. Which lessons—both academic and life lessons—are your children learning most from you right now?

Glossary of Key Terms

Academic & Homeschooling Terms

Assessment: The process of evaluating a child's learning, skills, or progress. Can include tests, portfolios, or informal observations.

Block Scheduling: A method of organizing the day into longer periods dedicated to specific subjects or activities.

Charlotte Mason Method: An educational philosophy emphasizing literature, nature study, narration, and short, focused lessons.

Classical Education: A traditional method focusing on the trivium (grammar, logic, rhetoric) and historical context in learning.

Eclectic Approach: Choosing elements from various educational philosophies and curricula to create a custom homeschooling plan.

Homeschool Co-op: A cooperative group of families who share teaching responsibilities, classes, or activities.

Independent Study: A flexible learning approach where the student works individually with guidance from the parent or tutor.

Lesson Plan: A detailed outline of what will be taught and how each lesson will be delivered.

Learning Styles: The preferred ways in which a child learns best, e.g., visual, auditory, kinesthetic, or hands-on.

Montessori Method: An approach emphasizing hands-on, self-directed learning and independence.

Narration: A method where a child retells or summarizes what they learned, often used in Charlotte Mason homeschooling.

Portfolio: A collection of a child's work that shows learning progress over time.
Project-Based Learning (PBL): Learning through engaging in projects that require critical thinking, research, and hands-on work.

Screen Time Balance: Managing technology use to support learning while avoiding overexposure or fatigue.

Unit Study: A teaching approach that explores one topic across multiple subjects, integrating learning for deeper understanding.

Chronic Illness & Energy Management Terms

Chronic Illness: A long-term health condition that may affect energy, mobility, or daily functioning.

Flare-Up / Flare Day: A period of increased symptoms or fatigue associated with chronic illness.

Pacing: Planning activities to prevent overexertion and conserve energy.

Restorative Breaks: Short periods of rest designed to restore energy and focus during learning or caregiving.

Spoon Theory: A metaphor for measuring and managing daily energy, especially for people with chronic illness. Each "spoon" represents a unit of energy.

Self-Care: Intentional practices to maintain physical, emotional, and spiritual well-being.

Energy Audit: An assessment of how much energy daily tasks consume to help plan manageable routines.

Adaptive Tools: Devices or strategies to make learning or daily tasks easier for children or parents with limitations.

Caregiver Burnout: Physical, emotional, and mental exhaustion from long-term caregiving responsibilities.

Parenting & Emotional Health Terms

Attachment Parenting: Parenting approach focused on strong emotional bonds, responsiveness, and nurturing relationships.

Emotional Resilience: The ability to adapt to stress and adversity while maintaining emotional balance.

Growth Mindset: Believing that intelligence and abilities can be developed through effort and learning.

Mindful Parenting: Practicing awareness, presence, and intentionality in interactions with children.

Positive Reinforcement: Encouraging desired behavior through praise, rewards, or acknowledgment.

Socialization: The process of learning to interact with others, develop friendships, and understand social norms.

Trust-Based Learning: Allowing children to explore and learn at their own pace with guidance and encouragement rather than strict control.

Administrative & Planning Terms

Transcripts: Official records of courses, grades, and credits, often required for high school or college admissions.

Graduation Plan: A roadmap of coursework and credits needed to complete high school at home.

Record-Keeping: The practice of tracking attendance, grades, assignments, and portfolios for compliance or personal reference.

Flexible Schedule: A plan that allows variation day-to-day to accommodate health, energy levels, and family needs.

Outsourcing: Hiring tutors, enrolling in online courses, or using external resources for subjects parents cannot teach themselves.

Annual Review: Evaluating the past year of homeschooling to adjust curriculum, goals, or strategies for the next year.

Resources

Homeschool Support Communities
- Facebook Groups: Homeschooling with Chronic Illness, Warrior Moms Homeschool Support
- Local homeschool co-ops (many offer scholarships or sliding-scale fees)
- Local libraries or community centers offering classes or activities

Online Curriculum & Learning Platforms
- Time4Learning
- Khan Academy
- Outschool
- Coursera (for high school/college-level enrichment)

Books to Inspire & Guide You
- The Brave Learner by Julie Bogart
- Teaching from Rest by Sarah Mackenzie
- The Read-Aloud Family by Sarah Mackenzie
- The Well-Trained Mind by Susan Wise Bauer
- Homeschooling for Chronic Illness by Dr. Heather MacDonald

Podcasts for Encouragement & Ideas
- The Homeschool Sisters Podcast
- Your Morning Basket
- Raising Lifelong Learners

- The Warrior Mom Guides Podcast (coming soon)

Printable Tools & Templates
- Daily logs, planners, and checklists (see Chapter 45)
- Lesson planners and goal trackers
- Emergency plans and low-energy schedules

The Warrior Mom's Guide™ Book Series

FOUNDATION: The Pilot Book

🤍 A Warrior Within, A Chronic Illness

The Warrior Mom's Guide to Sickle Cell & Chronic Resilience

My story of battling sickle cell while raising a family—woven with practical mindset shifts, survival tools, and advocacy.

📖 The heart of the Warrior Mom movement and the introduction to the series.

THE DEEP-DIVE SERIES (Books 1–10)

🤍 **The Warrior Mom's Guide to GhettoOCD™**

(Home Organization & Cleaning)

Practical, real-life homemaking strategies for moms with chronic illness.

❀ The Warrior Mom's Guide to Mental Wellness & Finding Joy in the Chaos

Therapy, prayer, and emotional survival tools for weary moms.

♥ The Warrior Mom's Guide to Single Motherhood by Choice

Reclaiming peace, health, and wholeness after carrying it all.

♥ The Warrior Mom's Guide to Loving Unexpectedly

Guardianship, Fostering & Adoption with Faith and Fierce Love

Finding your voice, courage, and confidence in nontraditional motherhood.

♥ The Warrior Mom's Guide to Generational Wealth & Family Legacy

Building wealth, purpose, and a future that lasts.

♥ The Warrior Mom's Guide to Spiritual Reset & Chronic Faith

Faith after diagnosis, grace during flare-ups, and spiritual renewal when you feel forgotten.

● **The Warrior Mom's Guide to ZBB & Cash Stuffing** (Finances)

Zero-based budgeting & cash envelope systems for sick-day survival.

🌿 **The Warrior Mom's Guide to Homeschooling for the Homegirls**

Practical tools for rest, rejuvenation, and chronic-illness-friendly homeschooling.

🖤 **The Warrior Mom's Guide to Homeownership & Stability**

Creative paths to securing a home with chronic illness and limited income.

🌿 **The Warrior Mom's Guide to Living in Peace**

End-of-life planning with grace: wills, medical directives, legacy projects, and restoration.

Find the books, companion workbooks, journals, planners, and more at:
www.warriormomacademy.com

Acknowledgments

To every warrior mom teaching her children from the couch, the hospital bed, or the kitchen table—I see you.

To my children, thank you for growing with me and being my "why" for every lesson learned and every challenge overcome.

To every mother just beginning this journey: you are not alone. You are joining a sisterhood of resilience and love.

This book is the result of having chronic faith, in myself and in the Father. With years of support, encouragement, and inspiration from my children.

Thank you to my family, the many homeschooling moms who shared their stories, and my editor, designer, and mentors for helping shape these words into a helpful guide.

And most of all, thank you—to you, the reader—for trusting me to walk alongside you. You are not alone.

About the Author

Shaundra M. G. Harris is a single mother, chronic illness advocate, and homeschooling mentor.

Drawing from her own journey of balancing motherhood, health challenges, and education, she empowers families to build joyful, sustainable homeschool lives.

Through practical strategies, faith-centered encouragement, and community support, she inspires moms to embrace their unique path with strength and grace.

Connect with Shaundra and explore more resources, journals, and companion materials at

www.warriormomacademy.com

www.ingramcontent.com/pod-product-compliance
Lightning Source LLC
Chambersburg PA
CBHW021157160426
43194CB00007B/783